DO IT BIG!

DO IT BIG!

The Power of Living with Crazy Faith!

"If the dream is big enough, the odds don't matter."

- Les Brown

Suze Guillaume

Build & Inspire Publishing
P.O. Box 681664
Miami, FL 33168

ISBN 978-0-996116138 (Paperback)
ISBN 978-0-996116121 (eBook)

www.suzeguillaume.com
info@suzeguillaume.com

Edited by Val Pugh
Cover Design by Grigoriu
Interior Design by Rosa_Penn

Ordering Information:
Quantity sales. Special discounts are available on quantity purchases by corporations, associations, and others. For details, contact the publisher at the address above.

Printed in the United States of America

First Edition

ACKNOWLEDGMENTS

For EJ, Iyhana, Hillary, Tania, and Benji:

Prayer is the greatest asset you have when growing your faith. When in doubt, pray!

For Mattine:

Thank you for giving me the permission to be free with my dreams. You are the true definition of black girl magic and we are creating doors in places that didn't have any before.

For Daddy:

Thank you for inspiring me and believing in me.

For Mommy:

You are my Haitian Queen, and this book is dedicated to you.

Men nou! Nou rive manman!

For my Sweet Jesus:

You made a way out of no way.

Thank you for giving me a second chance.

What is #CrazyFaith?

Crazy faith is when you simply refuse to let the odds against you stop you from believing what God can do in your life.

Believe in yourself.

Work for success.

Get things done.

Focus on one thing and master it.

Travel the world.

TAKE YOUR FAITH TO ANOTHER LEVEL!

Contents

Hello!

It's here!

Do it Big is finally here!

Can I say that the struggle is real?

Writing your own book is not easy.

Don't let anyone lie to you.

Not even me.

The process is painful.

I thought waking my 6-year-old son up at 6:00 a.m. to make it to school by 7:45 a.m. was painful. Don't get me wrong, waking him up *is* painful. Ask my sister Mattine. I call her every morning to complain. Actually, try it yourself. Try to wake him up, and then you will understand what I mean. Although I allow ample time for us to arrive at his school on time, we always seem to be late. I know when he gets to school, the Sister looks at us like, "Why are they always struggling to get here?" By the time we get to his school, they have already done the Morning Prayer. (*I know. I'm working on being better.*) Writing this book was an even a bigger struggle. Before getting started on it, I thought I had it together. You know those visions and dreams that you have for yourself, and you sit there fighting to get it done? Well, this book was one of those fights for me. With so many setbacks, never in a million years did I think that this day would come true. However, you are currently reading the vision that I literally spent ninety days hoping for. I'm not sure what I would be doing if I never completed this task. I'm not even sure whose life was waiting for this task to be completed. Still, I know one thing - the work is done, and it will continue.

I thought that I needed some magic powers to complete this book, but all I needed was my crazy faith, my laptop, my son, and my journey. I know that God only gives His strongest warriors the right battle to fight. I can remember being a kid dreaming of doing things that not every average kid was doing. I thought I had to look a certain way to be successful, but I'm currently living life without limits. I never thought that I would have a publishing company with my son. Yes, my business partner is a six-year-old kid who wants to travel the world, play sports, hang out with his aunt, practice baseball with his dad, and purchase the next Madden game that is coming out. Oh yeah, let me add that my kid is an award winning author. I know what you're thinking. *He is only six?* I said the same thing. (See, we think alike.) That's why he is my motivation for this book.

We as human beings are afraid to dream big. It's true. We only dream little enough to get us through the next day. We have to change that mentality, because we were not created to dream little, or be little. Our God is too big for errors, His ginormous graces are enough to go round, and round again! What is for you will be for you. I remember driving by big houses on the way to work thinking, *"Well, if I can just stare at the houses, maybe they can come to me."* Boy, was I wrong. I had no faith. The thing is, I've always been afraid. Growing up with Haitian parents, you better not dare express that you want to become a musician or a dancer. Musician who? Dancer what? These weren't considered real careers to Caribbean parents. It's not that our parents hated us. It's truly because the obstacles and challenges they faced as a children reflect how they raised their children. So bottom line, you better become a doctor or lawyer.

When you feel others don't support your dreams, I bet you tell yourself, "If others can't see me doing it, how can I see myself doing it?" Well, I'm here to tell you that what people think of you **DOESN'T MATTER**. I mean it. Let go of the people that are holding you back. Let them GO! Your time for a better life is now. God tells us over and over again that He will take care of us if we are obedient. Yet, we do the complete opposite. I was that girl. God would say one thing, and I would do something else. Clean out the negative people and things in your life, and start to make things happen. Dream big enough so you can work for it. Set goals so that you can hold yourself accountable. Now, with setting goals there will be a great deal of change in your life. We can't seem to see ourselves in a successful position; therefore, we settle for what society says we can have. On the contrary, what if there was an opportunity for you to be great? Give yourself a chance to raise the bar by creating opportunities for yourself and others around you.

Think about where you are in your life today. Are you where you thought you would be? What do you think of when I tell you to do it big? Are you afraid to live bigger? Are you afraid to fail? Write down five to ten fears that you may have. Next to each fear, write "You can't handle me."

_____

_____

_____

_____

_____

_____

_____

_____

_____

_____

_____

_____

_____

_____

CHAPTER 1
Unstoppable

Yes, I'm unstoppable.

I serve a God who is unstoppable.

Dreaming big is what every ambitious teenager does, at 19, I was already working in my career. However, at that age it's hard to get people to support you. After graduating high school, your parents want you to go to college and get an education. So, you go for it. Do you ever sit and ask yourself, what more can I offer myself? When you become the only person motivating yourself, you can get overwhelmed. The possibilities of your dreams will give you strength. How did I do it? I don't even know but I knew that I wanted more for myself. I got my first gig to work with MTV right after high school. I was a young college student working at the 2003 MTV Video Music Awards, and I was so excited. I remember my friends wouldn't believe me when I would tell them that I was working there with the VMAs. Here is a little secret,

1

sometimes you will have to move in silence. When you are silent about your moves, you become stronger. Clearly, they thought I was crazy, but I knew what I wanted out of life.

As I was going through my college years, I started an internship during the summer of my junior year at the University of Florida. The internship was at the Miami Beach Film & Print Office. At that Office, I was connected to everything happening in Miami. When I did my interview with the Office, I was determined. In fact, I called them like fifty times before I even got an interview. I will never forget Maya who did an interview with me. She asked why I was doing this - why was I interested in film and television. I told her that I wanted a better life for my mom. I didn't want my mom to work hard anymore. I remember that day vividly.

I was a young college student trying to DO BIG THINGS to literally change the way I was living. As we grow up, we absorb from our parents what success may look like. We are always looking for other people to validate our dreams. We always try to fit in and do what is normal. You have to get to a point where you know that you are unstoppable. If you know that you want to start an online magazine, do your research. Find out what you need to do to start the process. Later that week, I got a phone call from the Miami Beach Film & Print office, and they told me I got the job. Whoop! Whoop! I was jumping all over the place. However, they told me that it would not be a paying gig. I didn't know how I was going to explain no pay to my mom. Haitian parents don't understand that.

I was nervous because I had no money, but I knew the opportunity would change my outlook on life. I woke up every day with little to nothing to get to Miami Beach from Little Haiti. I never once thought that I could not make it. Every day when I woke up, I believed in myself that God had a plan for me. As a little twenty-year-old girl, I had access to every film project and music video that was being filmed in South Florida. See, most people will judge an opportunity by what the opportunity can offer them. I learned early in my career, to own the opportunity. It was bittersweet after I completed my internship months later, but I kept a contact of one of MTV's Production Coordinators. I didn't think calling them would work, but it did. Networking and following up is everything.

I got a Production Assistant lead job with the 2004 Video Music Awards. I found out later that day that I was only leading craft services. Yes, craft services. That meant that I was only head in charge of food for key people. (Don't laugh.) Although that was twelve years ago, that job was a significant start to my new life of possibilities. I took my role seriously, even though I was only serving coffee to the producers and handing boiled to eggs Kanye West and John Legend. You better believe that I was the best coffee and egg server ever! On top of that, I was making some mad cash, and I was happy. I share this story to tell you that there is power in contacts and networking. I was connected with so many people at a very young age. When you operate on crazy faith, the devil can't interfere. I am speaking from experience. He will definitely try to interfere, but the power of God is so grand. If you just call on His name, all kind of powers will begin to shift. Your faith can change your life with limited resources. Understand that you can do it big wherever you are with the resources you have. Also, remember that nothing happens by accident.

Your college years would be the best time to explore and take on big opportunities. (This message is for my grad students and doctoral students as well.) You can start a business right from your dorm room. Your buyers are already there with so many of the students getting financial aid refunds. Who cares if people think you are crazy? Regain your focus and operate on crazy faith. The early professional habits that I adapted while I was in college pushed me to be where I am today. You may be asking why now. Why not now? Procrastination only delays your success. What are some things you have been dreaming about doing but haven't started on it yet? On the lines below, write five goals that are wild enough to make you think you are crazy. Next, write five roadblocks that will hold you back from achieving those goals. Are you hungry enough to push through those roadblocks?

If you fail to plan, then you plan to fail. So start with the end in mind.

_____

_____

_____

_____

_____

_____

_____

_____

_____

_____

_____

_____

_____

_____

_____

_____

_____

_____

_____

_____

_____

_____

Five Crazy Faith Ideas

1. _____
_____
2. _____
_____
3. _____
_____
4. _____
_____
5. _____
_____

Five Roadblocks

1. _____
_____
2. _____
_____
3. _____
_____
4. _____
_____
5. _____
_____

Within the next week, connect with someone in your network that can help you start working on your idea. Always ask God for a sense of direction before doing anything. He will give you the answers. I promise. You can sit there and act like you have it all together if you want, or you can be unstoppable and change your life.

CHAPTER 2
Live Fearlessly

"You get in life what you have the courage to ask for."

Oprah Winfrey

When you realize your worth, you will never go back to past hurt, failures, mistakes, and distractions. You will see that everything you were going through was preparing you for your future. Accept the things you can control, and let go of the things you can't change. You can definitely control yourself and your attitude. I grew up learning that "Your attitude, not your aptitude, will determine your altitude." (Zig Ziglar) How far do you want to go in life? Where do you want to go? I never had answers to those questions. In fact, if you don't even have the answers, I understand. Still, until you move past your fears, you will be stuck in your ditch of disappointment. Keep in mind that no one can take you out of that ditch unless you realize that you deserve more in life. Once you come to that realization, you must move fearlessly towards your goal. To do so, you must let go of all negative feelings and negative people in your life. After that, prepare yourself to go to the next level. You have the power to change your circumstance when you enact your crazy faith. God never placed you on this earth to live in fear. So, stop everything you are doing at this very moment and say out loud, "I WAS BORN TO DO THIS!" Say it five more times. Whoop! Whoop! (I know I'm full of energy, but I'm just excited about what God is about to do for you.)

For example, take a look at children. If you have children pay attention to their actions and what they say. In fact, pay close attention to a baby who is learning how to crawl. Do you ever hear children say that they can't do something or they are afraid to do something? Kids are more likely to get hurt doing something they love. As adults, we know that we can get hurt doing something so we don't even try it. Other people's opinions of you are just that, they are opinions and not facts. Now, start putting positive things into the atmosphere. Let your voice resound as loud as you can. You can't allow your fear to have control of your mind. Let your faith determine how far you will go. I can only speak from my experience, but trust me when I tell you that crazy faith will get you farther than your wildest dream. Furthermore, your faith will shape your future.

There was a young girl who had big dreams of going to her dream college, the University of Florida. She was told not to apply because she wouldn't get accepted and she was also told to stay home in Miami because it would be best for her. She was passionate about her education. She knew if she went away that great things would happen for her. Before she heard back from UF she got over 7 rejection letters from different schools. Yes, even from state schools. Keep in mind she had the G.P.A., the test scores, and loads of community service hours. She was told by her own school counselor that college is not for everyone. Now, her counselor is right. She was a "B" average student with limited resources. Her parents weren't involved in the process because they didn't understand it. About two weeks before she made a decision to go to one of the local schools in her community she got two big packages in the mail. She got one package from New York University and one from the University of Florida. She got accepted to two big schools. That young girl was me. Yes, it was me. My parents' wouldn't allow me to go to New York University because it was too far but I got in to the University of Florida. This is when I realized my dreams were necessary.

Allow yourself to design where you want to go so that you can be exposed to more opportunities. If you always had a dream to start your own business or organization, your time is now. Take the time to focus on that idea. Create a plan for success. Then, allow it to manifest to the universe, and success will come looking for you. Keep in mind that, the universe will react to your next move, only if you move. Checkmate! If you want something, you have to go after it. Start by moving your ideas, and then live fearlessly with crazy faith.

Reflection:

Write down five things you want to do to live fearlessly.

_____

_____

_____

_____

_____

_____

_____

_____

_____

_____

_____

_____

_____

_____

_____

_____

_____

_____

_____

_____

CHAPTER 3
Impossible is Nothing

People who achieve big things are those who decide to try the things that seem impossible to others. We serve a big God.

Suze Guillaume

When you wake up in the morning do you ever take the time to tell yourself how great you are? Do you every wake up telling yourself that I'm going to give today my all. There are so many of us, including myself, we are so eager to get to where we have to go and we never make the time to self reflect. We don't. I know this may seem strange but do you? Yes, let that sink in for a little. Most of the times, people will share a quote on the Instagram or Facebook but not even apply the words they put out there to their own lives.

I remember waiting on my parents to help me make things happen. Yet, as I got older, I realized that having faith is free. I would ask my parents for stuff, and I would rarely get it. I would ask to do things like take dance classes, and I was always ignored. I thought the words *no* and *impossible* were like power words that people got paid to say. What I didn't realize was that, as human beings, we are immune to the word *impossible*. I dislike the word because it opens doors for our fears to come in and break us down. *Impossible* has not allowed us to live to our fullest potential. When I heard *no* so much from my parents, I really thought that nothing was possible. Therefore, I stopped asking them to take me to dance school and music school. Instead, I began to reach out to my school teachers to see if there were any programs at the school.

After being patient, I finally told my parents that I would sign up to join the school dance team for the upcoming school year. My mom looked at me and said, "Okay, but make sure the program director tells me your rehearsal time and so on." I thought to myself, *"Yes. I did it. My mom will let me go to the dance rehearsals."* Because I never gave up, my mother eventually gave in and allowed me to pursue my dream. I started to dance and act for my school's magnet program. It felt good to touch the stage, but I had to wonder about all the other kids who had dreams of dancing and acting. I wondered who or what was stopping them from achieving their goals. Whatever you do, make sure you get rid of the word *impossible* before you get started on anything. That word is so powerful, and it will shatter your dreams just like what it almost did to me. When you use that word, it can determine how far you will go in life.

If I would have listened to my parents, I would have never had the opportunity to dance and perform at the school. Today, I ask you to start new with the word *possible*. Parents, do the same for your children. Tell them that everything is possible, and impossible is nothing. Anything that they work hard for can become their reality. I made a promise to God to tell my son that the word *possible* would be his best friend. Furthermore, I promised that I would never allow him to think that he can't accomplish his goals in life. My parents came from Haiti with little to nothing. I could understand why they would tell me that I couldn't do much, but I also don't think that my parents knew the power of their words. You can speak things into existence. When I signed up for the dance program at my school, that is what exactly happened. I was able to let go of the word *impossible* and replace it with *faith* and *possible*. Give your kids the extra push they need to be successful. Just because things weren't perfect for you, doesn't mean your kids can't be successful. Parents tend to tune their children out because of their age, but you would be surprised what would happen if we listen to our children more. God actually uses children to help their parents. God is sometimes waiting on you to activate your faith, in fact, he is waiting for you now.

Truly I tell you, if you have faith as small as a mustard seed, you can say to this mountain, "Move from here to there," and it will move. Nothing will be impossible for you.

Matthew 17:20, The Bible
(New International Version)

Think of the things that are hindering you from activating your faith. This will allow you to see your setbacks. Hey, If God put me to work, he can put you to work as well. At the end of your list, write

"Nothing will be impossible for me."

_____
_____
_____
_____
_____
_____
_____
_____
_____
_____
_____
_____
_____
_____
_____

CHAPTER 4
Moving Your Ideas

Wake up out of your mess. Today.
Dust yourself off and move.
You may be wondering how to get your
ideas off the ground?
Well, you have to work for it..
It's that simple.

At the same time of moving your big ideas, set goals that are believable and achievable. Most people want to jump from 1 to 1,000 over night when 1 to 10 might be more reasonable. How many people do you know that want a great future but aren't willing to put in the time to get from 1 to 10. The mission is clear, you have put in the time. If you are working a full time job, MAKE THE TIME TO INVEST IN YOUR OWN IDEAS. You can start small with maybe a t-shirt line or even an online business. You can also start blogging online to draw people to your website.

Whatever it is, you have to work for it. You may have to put aside two hours every day to focus on that idea or that vision, but there needs to be some kind of commitment. The commitment has to be consistent. Moreover, in order to do big things, you need to believe that you can do big things.

This is why I love being in business with my son, because he doubts nothing. He says, "Let's do it," and we continue to move on the next idea. At times, it could be harder working with older people. It seems that the older we get, the more we doubt the possibilities of our Creator. We often like to sit back and wait for God to send us a miracle. Stop sitting around melting your head with bible verses and prayer when you are not even putting in the work for anything. I guarantee that if you invest in your ideas for the next three years, your life will never be the same. You will be so busy that people will be asking where you are and what are you doing. You have it in you to do it, so DO IT.

When you have a full time job, you invest at least seven and a half hours a day to do work for someone else that is not even moving your ideas. Here is the secret to that: Start using your work to benefit your future. Yes, I said it. This is how you can help your ideas and visions. Not many of us can leave our jobs realistically because we have children or a family to take care of, but you are not out of options. You can use the professional development workshops at your job to better you. You can take classes at a vocational school or technical school to develop some skills. Most jobs have benefits like tuition reimbursement. If you interact with people on a daily basis, treat them like your customers. These are skills you can develop on the job. Practice being on time and giving 100% every day, even if you don't want to do it. After work, commit to at least one to two hours to work on ideas, and always have your goals set before walking out the door.

To work on your ideas, you can create a daily checklist. You can use your tablet or simply gather your thoughts throughout the week. In order for your ideas to work, you must write them down. Once you have your ideas down, focus on one list per week. There is something about writing down your vision and watching it come to life. If you heed my advice, I guarantee there will be changes in your life. You can actually start making those changes now. Below, I want you to write down some ideas that you can bring to life. You can easily focus on one thing, or you can write down multiple things. Don't take your ideas with you to the grave, where they are of no use to anyone. You have to remember that great ideas are not just in some of us, it is deposited in everyone who cares to pay attention. It is one thing to have ideas, and it is yet another to put your ideas into motion and let them bear fruit. Let me share this verse with you from the book of Ecclesiastes:

If the clouds are fill of water, they pour rain upon the earth. Whether a tree falls to the South or to the North, in the place where it falls shall it remain.

There are things you want to do, you cannot say you've tried hard enough...you cannot afford to stop. In the arithmetic of persistence, there is no addition or multiplication.

Pick up your pen, and in a reflective mood, put down your ideas, and take action...

_____

_____

_____

_____

_____

_____

_____

_____

_____

_____

_____

_____

_____

_____

_____

_____
_____
_____
_____
_____
_____
_____
_____
_____
_____
_____
_____
_____
_____
_____
_____
_____
_____
_____
_____
_____
_____
_____
_____
_____
_____

CHAPTER 5

Prepared for Rejection!

No!
I'm so sick of that word,
but I love it at the same time.

This is where the real fun begins. It begins at No. This is where you get up and go harder. This is where you brush the *No* off and keep it moving. There are so many people that stay buried in a "no" or get upset if someone don't help them out. Your work is an act of service that you are being used for to deliver for people.

My son and I got told no at least fifty times when we started to write his first children's book. He was just five years old at the time. People told me that it was not possible and that I needed to focus on something else. What did they know? I was told that I need a publishing company to pick up my son's idea. Someone else told me that I needed to know how to write children's books. I was told that no one would air my story because I was not doing enough to give back the community. I was even told that black people don't really write books. I called so many people for help, and I got so many rejections. There were so many people that mentioned that they would help, but they never did anything. You have to realize quickly that your ideas are not about you. It's about the plan God have for you and the other people out there that need to be inspired by your visions.

Today, my son has won three children's book awards by the grace of God. What would have happened if I would have listened to the people that told me no? I learned that most people will not see the best thing for you, and the other people don't care. That's okay, because your dream is not meant for everyone to be part of or to know. Use your rejection as motivation to get your idea done. You can also believe that people have their own agenda.

You can't expect people to stop what they are doing to focus on you or to make your plans a priority. If you want something done, do it yourself and make it happen. Don't be afraid to take on challenges. Most people can't see past their environment. When you are moving on an idea, keep in mind that you have to stay focused, humbled, and ready for all trials. Furthermore, maintain positive thoughts, because your mind will give you exactly what you ask for.

Remember that rejections are designed to keep you from reaching your goals. In fact, they are a part of your path to success, and you can't expect people to help you. If I would have focused heavily on the denials, I would not have made it to where I am today. There was a news station that I called constantly to air my son's story. I believe they denied me like ten times until we finally got a call from the news station telling us that they wanted to air our story. At that point, I wasn't surprise because I knew that the mind over matter theory was working, and God was creating opportunities on His time. I knew that if I kept my mind on what was important, God would continue to make my son's story relevant.

Your ideas are your gifts to the world. You never know whose life will be transformed from your assignment, so get to work and stop making excuses. The most valuable asset that you have right now is your faith. This is something that you will learn as you move your ideas. Value your ideas as blessed treasures from God. This is called an assignment that you were given to change lives. When you disregard the idea, you become the individual that is allowing the universe to suffer in silence. Some people are so afraid of rejection, but you have to become immune to rejection. This skill is essential for when you start asking friends and family to support your movement. Accept the fact that not everyone will understand your mission, even with a mission statement. Simply continue to move on your ideas, and watch the manifestation of your dreams. You are about to create your own doors of opportunities.

Think of positive words you can use when someone tell you no. Write them down because you will definitely need them to keep you focused.

_____

_____

_____

_____

_____

_____

_____

_____

_____

_____

_____

_____

_____

_____

_____

_____

_____

_____

_____

_____

_____

_____

_____

_____

_____

_____

_____

_____

_____

_____

_____

_____

_____

_____

_____

_____

_____

_____

_____

_____

_____

_____

Support EJ's Literacy World by purchasing the book series at: www.suzeguillaume.com

CHAPTER 6

Bigger Than Your Dreams

"The reason birds can fly and we can't is simply because they have perfect faith, for to have faith is to have wings."

J.M. Barrie, *The Little White Bird*

At what point in your life will you decide that it is time to make a change in your life? When will you start believing in things that you can't see? So many people are so caught up in their dreams that they don't ever see progress with their ideas or visions. Well, you can't expect your idea to just move on its own. A successful person will not just dream about success. They will work for it. They will find ways that will not work and continue to put it more work to get the job done. Your visions have to be for a cause larger than yourself, and you have to be willing to put in work. Some people can only see what is in front of them, but I dare you to start believing in the impossible. I dare you to start believing in what you can't see. I dare you to simply have faith.

Unfortunately, as a kid, most of our dreams are shut down by the age of five. That's the most crucial time of a child's life, and parents don't realize that because most of their dreams were shut down. Now, it's time to forget about the time your dream was shattered. You have to be bigger than your dreams. You can't just imagine things will be a certain way for the rest of your life. You have dream even bigger than you did at such a young age, and you have to work for success. Furthermore, you have to become more disciplined to get it done. Most people want the dream to come to life over night, but life doesn't work that way. I recently learned to look at things intently. According to the Webster Dictionary, the word *intently* means that you have to look at your visions with "earnest and eager attention." Simply put, you have to stare your vision down to the point where you know what you want.

Not everyone can be on this journey with you. Most people don't even move on their own dreams unless their dreams are validated by people who haven't accomplished anything in their entire life. The worst thing you can do is ask someone if your dream makes sense to them.

You don't need validation from anyone to complete your assignment. The title of the book is *Do It Big*. That doesn't mean that you should sit around and feel bad for yourself. It means you should take that big idea one step at a time and achieve your massive goal.

The greatest gift you can give to yourself is the gift of consistency. That is to plan accordingly every day with your ideas and visions. Yet, be prepared for hiccups along the way. Don't think for a second that you will be free from problems. A person with a focused mind will face challenges daily. Just view the problems as a necessary step towards achieving your goal. Your dreams and lessons are necessary, but that is only if you believe that. The crazy thing is, sometimes we are walking pass our vision every day without feeding it and nurturing it. Meanwhile, our vision is dying of thirst and nourishment. Think about a plant that is dry and needs water. Could you imagine what that plant is going through? How do you think your visions and idea feels when you disregard it? Do you know how many people are waiting for you to share your story or your journey?

Some people sit in their mess for so long that they give other people around them the opportunity to live their dream. No one around you is going to push you harder than yourself - not even your parent or closest friend. No one is going to believe the idea for you. Most successful people excel because they become that dream or idea. You have to put that dream to work when you are planning, negotiating, focused, and consistent. People always ask how I did it. They want to know how I got to this point in my life. I simply tell them that I just worked on my dream while I maintain my nine to five job. Although the responsibilities of the job sometimes hindered my chances of working towards my dream, I continued to plan accordingly. I would dedicate my lunch breaks to networking and editing. Most of the time, I didn't have the time to edit and network, but I had a schedule that worked for me. Was it difficult? Yes, it was. However, every time I wanted to give up there, was a voice that told me to keep going. You have to create the time to work on your dreams. Think of the best time of the day that you can make it happen. Is it during your lunch break or in the evening after work? Below, think of the days and times that will work for you. You will only know if you can write it down. There are too many of us waiting on our big break but not willing to work to bring the vision to life. This particular dilemma is for entrepreneurs. You want to plan a conference for your business but you never made the time to plan it. Pick up your pen and write down the best times for you to work on your dreams. Be consistent and be sure to have an accountability partner.

The Best Days and Time for me to work on my Dreams are:

_____

_____

_____

_____

_____

_____

_____

_____

_____

_____

_____

_____

_____

_____

_____

_____

The best day and time for me to work on my dreams are:

_____

_____

My accountability partner is:

_____

CHAPTER 7

Passport Ready:

Always Be Prepared, Even When You Are Not!

Being passport ready will never fail you if you trust the process and trust your journey. So many people dream so big and never get to achieve anything. Are you passport ready? Do you have a passport? Have you ever thought about traveling the world? Aren't you tired of being in the box that held you captive for years? Will you be ready when that unexpected phone call requires you to travel outside of the country? Always be prepared for an opportunity that you don't even know about. I tell my friends that it is important to be prepared without knowing what you are being prepared for. This is called being passport-ready. So, if you don't already have a passport, get it done and do not procrastinate.

I learned the importance of having a passport at an early age when I was given an opportunity to visit Haiti to help with the development of a new school. Actually, I wasn't ready when they contacted me, because I didn't have a passport. Therefore, I had to rush to get the passport within two weeks, and I didn't even have the money to spend. The organization contacted me and asked if I would join them on a mission trip to help build a playground and school for children in a small village. I wasn't sure if I was ready to pack my bags and go into a country that I wasn't familiar with, but I thought of the blessings and opportunities that were waiting for me if I took the chance to prepare to travel with these leaders. What would I lose, or what would I gain? I realized that I really had nothing to lose at all. Actually, I started to fall in love again with my parent's country. Haiti is still and will always be beautiful. The children there are so happy. I learned to appreciate life through this journey as well.

There was one morning when I woke up in the village that made me see things differently. I took a shower and headed out to do missionary work. I was in charge of preparing the juice for breakfast. I had a bag of sugar that I was carrying with me, but I didn't realize the there was a hole in the bag. After I noticed the hole, I quickly grabbed a bowl to put the sugar in and noticed that the kids in the village were behind me. When I looked back, I could only shed tears because the children were eating the sugar from the ground. My heart was hurting to see the children eating the sugar like that. I didn't realize that this trip to Haiti would open up my eyes to the reality of this world. After spending eight days in the Fund Lecture, Port de Paix, I realized something quite valuable in life. Based on that experience, I made up my mind to always be passport-ready.

What's the most critical ingredient to living your dreams? It's your mindset. You control the birth of your ideas. Find your passion and work for success. When you know what you want, it will motivate you to produce. Be prepared for the unexpected and always be ready for an opportunity. I used to get upset when someone didn't give me a chance to do something, but I realized as I got older that whatever God has for you will be for you - no one can stop that. Being prepared for an opportunity means to be forward thinking and to give everything your best. What if I missed the opportunity to visit Haiti two years ago? What if I decided that I couldn't afford a passport? Maybe there is an opportunity for you to get involved with a project that you believe will help you with your growth process, well do it. Research places you would like to visit, and always be passport ready. Your time might be coming sooner than expected. Being a continuous explorer is something that will keep you energized because learning something new or going to a different place around the world will ignite something in you.

Reflection:

Name five (5) places that you would like to visit within the next five (5) years. It can be anywhere around the world. List three (3) organizations that you can work with at each destination. Also, start working on getting your passport. You never know when an opportunity will come to change your life ☺.

_____

_____

_____

_____

_____

_____

_____

_____

_____

_____

_____

_____

_____

_____

_____

_____

_____

Turn your struggles into passport stamps!

CHAPTER 8

Step Out of Your Comfort Zone

*"All I have seen teaches me to trust the
Creator for all I have not seen."*

Ralph Waldo Emerson

Have you ever tried to do something that made you feel uneasy? Have you ever tried to do something you never tried before? How did you feel after trying it out? Never in a million years did I think that I could write a book. In fact, I laughed at myself because I just didn't think it was possible. This very book you are reading is a miracle. Did I think it was possible? Yes. Did I know I can do it? No. I was scared for my life, but it was an assignment that I had to complete. I know you are probably thinking that in order for you to be prepared, you need to first know what you are doing. Oh no! I wish success would work out that way. I didn't know who to talk to about my plans. I was clueless. I started researching and found some programs to help me understand the world of self-publishing. I was too comfortable with where I was at in my life, and I needed more. Even though I was clueless, I knew that I could do more. I encouraged myself. Sometimes you have to stand up and tell yourself that you can do it.

When you are close to something great, doubt and fear tend to creep into your mind. Then, challenges and difficulties arise. This makes the finish line even harder to reach. Still, you must press forward with your dreams while leaping over hurdles and obstacles. Some people have dreams of starting their own mentoring service, developing a reading program for the youth, starting a restaurant, or becoming mayor of their city. Yet, they never research ways to get started because they lack faith in themselves. How will you know where to start if you never even begin learning the process? The greatest asset that you have is your faith. In this book, we talk about crazy faith because you have to start believing in things you can't see. You have to start seeing the things to come. Our vision can become so blurry when we watch television or the morning news that if we look at our surroundings, we can become extremely blind to the fact that we have work to do.

Your dream is not even about you anymore. It's about those kids who are hanging out on the street corner. It's for a single mother who is living off of the government with no additional income. It could also be for that little boy who grew up without his mom or dad. If you think your dream is only about you, then this book is not for you. *Do It Big* is to inspire that one person to change the world and their community. We have to step out of our own comfort zone working that nine to five and do more work outside of what we are told to do. You can give 100% to your job every day by waking up, getting to work on time, building vacation days to take that next vacation, planning events at work, and giving your customers 100% customer service. However, you can't even invest time for your business and your organization. Yes, it will take extra hard work, sleepless nights, endless phone calls, banging on people's doors, and sacrificing certain lifestyles, but it will work.

Everything that you were assigned to do is your responsibility to get it done. You can allow someone to control the outcome of your day, or you can start controlling your destiny and your legacy. Start to preserve the very legacy that God promised to be yours. I know it's hard to let go of things that you are so accustomed to doing, but I guarantee that you will never know the power you have over your life until you get up, dress up, get out, and challenge yourself. Moreover, you will never know how far you can go until you try to give your best every day. I am challenging you today to start something new and move with the power of crazy faith. I did so in 2004, when I got the job opportunity that changed my life. The production coordinator said he needed an assistant to complete craft services such as making coffee, warming bagels, and making boiled eggs. So, I went over to his desk and told him that I would do it. He looked at me and smiled. Then, he told me that I would go really far in life. I was hungry anyway, and if I was in charge of the food, I would be able to eat it as well.

I took on the challenge for about two weeks, and it was the best experience ever. I realized two things: the producers will be your best friend, and the celebrities will always remember you. I learned quickly how to develop meaningful relationships while serving food. I didn't just see my role as the food server. I saw myself with an opportunity. After that, the producer of the show I was working on became my mentor. He was hard on me though, and I wasn't sure that I could handle him, but I did. I mastered the producer of the show because I knew what time he wanted coffee, how he liked his coffee, and I knew the very thing that would make him mad. I kept myself out of his radar but on top of his needs. I learned from him how to be ten steps ahead of the opponent without letting the opponent know. Furthermore, he always told me that time is money and that every second counts on television. I had the opportunity to learn all of this at the age of twenty-one.

I had celebrities come and tell me that I made the best boiled eggs, and you better believe that I did. John Legend and Kanye West were recording a video at the time. I will never forget that experience. They walked with an entourage and my craft service table was close to them. They stopped at my table and ate about four boiled eggs. I was one proud sister! It didn't matter that my job was dealing with food and people. What matters is that I learned from doing the things that people do not want to do. I was afraid of failing because I knew that I would have the opportunity to connect with people. At least I can say that I made boiled eggs for some top people. What opportunities are you turning down because you think you are better than that request? It's all about being at the right place at the right time and taking advantage of opportunities.

When you start doing things that make you uncomfortable, you start to find your real talents with endurance. I want you to think of three things that you would never do. Write them below. Then, complete those tasks and write the dates of completion. Select one thing you would challenge yourself to do this year. It doesn't have to be anything big. Tell yourself how you can use that one thing to your advantage. You don't have to tell anyone about this exercise, but I want your faith to go to another level. If I didn't take on that responsibility of working at the craft services table, I would have never met the producers on the show. They were not the nicest people in the world, but I wasn't looking for a friendship nor was I looking for a relationship. I was only looking for an opportunity to learn anything from the industry. What permission are you giving to your fears to mobilize them?

Write out those things that scare you the most, and then write out an action plan to get out of your comfort zone, the zone of stagnation!

_____

_____

_____

_____

_____

_____

_____

_____

_____

_____

_____

_____

_____

_____

_____

_____

_____

_____

_____

_____

CHAPTER 9

Be Consistent

*"Each day, focus your attention on
what you want. Each day, take one step
that will bring you closer to it."*

Iyanla Vanzant

S tay on top of your grind. Don't let a moment go by
without you grinding. If you are at a special event,
network and connect with people. Don't just stand there. At
every event, I try my best to take advantage of that very
moment. You never know who you will meet. Be consistent
with everything you do. Read books that relate to your
interest. This is another lesson I learned because I was always
sitting around praying without doing much work towards
my goals. God doesn't want us to sit around and wait for
Him to do things for us. This is where we are confused. God
want us to work and connect with people that will help us
complete our goals. Being consistent will allow you to grow

and develop relationships. Consistency allows you to be disciplined.

I am grateful for all of my experiences. At an early age, I knew what made me happy. When I was fourteen years old, I made up my mind that I wanted to be an actress. I loved performing and being on stage, and I was determined to make my dream come true. I was eventually featured on a TV show in Miami, and I was traveling doing stage plays. I enjoyed doing it. I made sure to attend every rehearsal, and I reviewed my script every day until I had every line down. I was consistent and determined. When my parents saw me on stage for the first time, they were so proud of me. It made me so happy to see them there.

When you have dreams or ideas, you have to support them by being consistent and determined to accomplish that task or goal. There are so many people with great ideas, but they are not consistent with getting the work done to accomplish the goal. Being consistent will give you the will power to complete the assignment needed to meet your goals. Realize that not everyone will support your vision. Actually, be mindful of the people who you share your ideas with.

Think of ways where you can be consistent with your dreams. What will push you to follow through on your assignments? Write down a few things that will allow you to be consistent with your dreams. If you are trying to go back to school, what will help you meet that goal?

_____

_____

_____

_____

_____

_____

_____

_____

_____

_____

_____

_____

_____

_____

_____

_____

_____

_____

_____

_____

*"I realized that I have to stop sharing
my million-dollar dreams with hundred-
dollar people."*

Steve Harvey

CHAPTER 10
Take Risks

"Do one thing every day that scares you."

Eleanor Roosevelt

In the world we live in today, we often find ourselves waiting for someone to cheer us on through a like or a Facebook message. We are always waiting on someone validate what we are doing. We are always waiting for someone to give us a hand out. Take a risk on yourself. Believe in you. Stand in your faith! Move in this moment from optional to non-negotiable.

Last year, I learned that if I maximize every hour in my day and use the hours properly, I will be closer to my goals. God blessed me with a full day to meet my goals. How I spend it and who I spend it with will determine how successful I will be. I learned that I need to hustle through my day and take more chances. Hence, I make phone calls to organizations that are hosting events and see how I can benefit and build my program. Do big things so you can blow away small minds. Take chances and risks. You don't have a lot of room for errors and negative people, so put more time into what you deserve in life.

God will share visions with you, but you have to come up with a plan to get there. Don't expect Him to do the work for you, because it won't happen that way. During my internship at the Miami Beach Film & Print Office with my current mentor, Maya, I had the opportunity to learn about her visions. At the age of twenty-two, I didn't understand what she was really saying, but I still committed it to memory. She mentioned to me that she was going to start her own farm. I wondered if she could really do it and if she had enough money to do it, but I loved the idea. However, I thought that I was about to lose the one person that believed in me. Maya always talked about doing big things. Keep in mind, she had a family at the time, but that never changed her focus. She really believed that she was going to start her own farm.

When she shared her vision with me back in 2005, I was about to graduate from college. Last year in 2015, I went to visit Maya and her family in Orlando, FL. I had to go see her because I missed her. When I arrived at her home, there was the farm that she dreamed about for years. The fierce color of green was everywhere, and I was witnessing the vision that was birthed almost ten years ago. She first spoke the farm into existence, and there it was. There were animals and crops everywhere. My son was eating celery and romaine lettuce from the farm. She even created a place where people can come and get fresh foods. This was another part of her vision. Maya had a job back in Miami and was living a comfortable life, but she took her savings and her crazy faith to Orlando and started a farm. She lives on the farm, and she has yoga classes there, too. In addition, she invites schools to come on field trips with children. What a risk she was able to take! She moved herself and her family to a different place to start a farm that she dreamed about to help other people have access to fresh food.

Have you ever had a dream that you thought was a risk? Have you ever had a vision that made you scared for your life? Take that risk. You may not think it's the right time, but there is no perfect timing. God's timing is the only time that is perfect. He wants the best for us, but we have to see it for ourselves. Maya may not know the impact she had on my life. The same woman at the Miami Beach Film & Print Office that took a chance with me made me realize that I can dream big and work for success. She invested in me and taught me everything that I needed to know about the production industry. This is the same woman that shared her dreams with me. She worked for her dreams, and she put her vision to work. Now, she is the proud owner of Maya Papaya Organic Farm in Oveido, FL. She left a full time job, saved up what she had, and purchased a property to start a farm.

See, there are only twenty-four hours in a day. If you use them wisely, you can put your dreams to work. If you control the information you put out and the information that you take in, you can control your visions. Sometimes you don't even know it, but your risks and blessings are working in your favor -even if they seem far from reality. You just have to make things happen. Don't wait until things are not ideal. You have to decide to act and move now. There will be times when you want to give up, but your reason for starting will get you back on track. Don't waste your time focusing on the things you don't have. The possibilities are endless when you work for success. You don't see the results now, but they will come. This is the only moment you have to make things better and to get the life you deserve.

We forget so quickly the power God has given to us. God has trusted you with the power to change your circumstances. In return, you have to dedicate yourself to achieve your goals. Your dreams are worth caring for. My experiences are what have given me a chance to live and breathe again. When you realize that everything around you is made up by people that are no smarter than you, you will then realize your power.

Do what you have to do every day to get to where you are going. Develop habits of success that will be the building blocks of your risks. God will see you through even when you are not trying for yourself.

You don't need to be ready for risks, because all you need is your crazy faith and your power of believing that all things are possible with your Creator. Wake up, pray, and keep going hard even when you are too tired to even move. Not every risk will be successful, but the risk you take will open doors and give you a chance at a better life. You don't need validation from anyone to be successful. When your family is asleep, go hard and pray harder. Push yourself harder every day. Give yourself permission to be great, and fly as high as you can. When it rains, go harder. You are your own motivation. God gave you enough strength to take on the challenges that you are going to face. You are in control of your thought process. Be great, move with courage, ask God for guidance, and take risks.

What risks are you willing to take this year? Write them down, and do it big! There is nothing too hard for God. You got this! What risks are you willing to take this year? It doesn't have to be anything big. Maybe you want to take small steps to obtaining a $30,000 loan for your business. You have to start somewhere. Take some time to think of the risks that you are willing to take this year to make necessary changes on your life. Choose a quiet place for this assignment. Turn off all gadgets and clear your mind. Give God some time to send some answers to your way. Don't be afraid to dream big.

What risks am I willing to take, and how I will benefit.

_____

_____

_____

_____

_____

_____

_____

_____

_____

_____

_____

_____

_____

_____

_____

_____

_____

_____

_____

_____

Support Maya Papaya Organic Farm by visiting: www.mayapapaya.com

CHAPTER 11
Get Uncomfortable

"Pain is temporary. Quitting lasts forever."

Lance Armstrong, *Every Second Counts*

Yes, repeat that title of this chapter again… Get uncomfortable. If your dream is to become a motivational speaker, you have to visualize yourself as that person. You have to think about what you will wear on stage with the latest fashion. You have to start thinking about how you want your audience to welcome you. The things that will make you uncomfortable you have to start thinking about them now.

Take about 3-5 minutes to think about all of those awesome ideas you had and you didn't act on them because you really had no one to support you. Now, think about the times that you invested so much time helping someone else's dreams come true. You put all of your efforts into someone else, but you never invest the time into your own ideas. I know. The thinking process can be painful. I'm not saying to not support other people, but what about your dreams? What about you? Some people are so comfortable in other people's dreams that they completely forget what their purpose is or what it will ever be. GET UNCOMFORTABLE.

That was me for several of years. I loved helping people and people loved me back. That was it. They loved me and admired my work ethic. I don't ever think I had anyone ask me about my visions and goals. Yes, that's hurtful, but you can't depend on people to make your dreams come true. I remember telling myself that I don't want to leave this earth with all of my ideas buried away. You have to say the same for yourself.

I can tell you that God used my son to make me very uncomfortable. After we launched my son's first book, people were asking us to come and speak. Let me add that he was getting paid to speak to people. Let's talk about small business doing big things! He was bold and outspoken. On the other hand, I was so scared, but my son had no fears. He was always ready to speak. One time, we had to speak to a fairly small group of kids. However, when we arrived, there were over four hundred people seated in one room. The kids were there with their parents. All I can think was that we were about to embarrass ourselves. I didn't like public speaking. Nevertheless, I went into a corner with my son, said a prayer, and asked EJ if he was ready. He stood there and said, "Of course, Mom. I'm ready to get paid. We got this."

Keep in mind that I was that same little girl who used to perform in front of large crowds. However, I had become so comfortable with being behind the scenes that I was terrified of people and what they would think of me. When I would prepare to go on stage, I would look out at the audience and imagine that the parents would say rude things about me. Well, guess what? After the presentation, there were parents and kids running up to us saying that we motivated and inspired them. I looked over at my son thanked him for making me so uncomfortable. We did it! We did it! We even sold all of the books that we had available.

Are you uncomfortable yet? What will it take to make you believe in yourself? Are you ready to step out on crazy faith? Do you believe that you can do big things with the resources you currently have? We serve an amazing God, so let's go. I want you to get uncomfortable this year. Leave the small thinking behind. Start making phone calls to people that can help you meet your goals. You have it in you to be great. Settling for mediocrity is not what God wants for you. Write down five things that make you uncomfortable and next to each item write how you change that one thing that makes you uncomfortable. Be sure to listen to your kids because they may be the ones to inspire you. As you write down your ideas, think of where you see yourself? What life challenges are you ready to face? What makes you so uncomfortable that will push you to move on your visions?

_____

_____

_____

_____

_____

_____

_____

_____

_____

_____

_____

_____

_____

_____

_____

_____

_____

_____

_____

_____

_____

_____

_____

_____

_____

_____

_____

_____

_____

_____

_____

_____

_____

*The moment you make a command to
the Universe for something that serves your
highest good- and then you get into action
creating it- the Universe aligns with your
request and begins to move that very desire
in your direction.*

Lisa Nichols

CHAPTER 12

Not So Easy

*"What you must learn to do, you learn
by doing."*

Aristotle

If you think this journey is ice cream and cupcake, stop what you are doing. There's no need to focus on any of your ideas, because you are setting yourself up for disappointments. You see, if you are going to move on your ideas and visions, it will not be an easy road. You will have to do more work and not get paid to see the results. If someone tells you that you are in it to get paid in the first two to five years of business, they are lying. You will probably spend more money out of your own pocket before you can see results.

Remember, not everyone will support your ideas or your initiatives. Not everyone will understand your journey. Your journey is not meant for everyone to understand. Your supporters will be people you don't know. Your supporters will be the people who are interested in your product or what you have. Don't expect your family and friends to be loyal or committed to your project. Move with what you have and who you have. Furthermore, don't get offended if someone you thought would support you doesn't.

The most difficult part about an entrepreneur's journey is keeping your faith during difficult times. It's going to get tough. So if you are not ready to take a leap out on crazy faith, stay exactly where you are. Don't try anything new, because you will get disappointed. Leave it to someone who is prepared for the battle. If you can't go through the storm, be still and stay comfortable. Actually, when you start moving on your ideas you will realize your strengths and weaknesses. These are things you want to know because no one will inform you of them. At your job, you can have performance reviews, but it's not the same when you realize your own potential. Your journey will allow you to test your trials and tribulations. Your strengths will complete your weaknesses and shape them to their full potential.

In addition, you will have to learn early to tune people out. The human spirit is powerful. You can control your thoughts, your emotions, your feelings, and your money through your spirit. How will you know that you are doing your best if you're holding on tightly to things that are keeping you from going anywhere? How will you know the power you have if you continue to doubt yourself? Sometimes we doubt ourselves so much that we doubt ourselves out of our assignment and someone else's blessing. Meanwhile, someone will hop on it and move with your idea. People are waiting for you to fail so they can hop on the very thing that pushed and motivated you in the first place. If you want it, you have to work for it.

- ❖ Pray and ask God for direction.

- ❖ Start writing down your ideas.

- ❖ Place your ideas on a vision board.

- ❖ Connect with three people that can help you move your idea.

- ❖ Set timelines and deadlines.

- ❖ Network like crazy.

- ❖ Build Relationships.

- ❖ Eliminate Self-Doubt.

Keeping in mind all the items listed above will get you to start moving on initiatives. Your community is a great place to begin. Let's say you are passionate about policies and decision-making for your community. Get to know your City Commissioners and learn more about what they do and how it can benefit your ideas. Attend City Hall meetings to become aware of things affecting your community. Maybe you want to start a program for homeless or foster youth. Find a local organization, and partner up. It is a lot easier to start learning from someone who is already involved with the process. Your goal is to understand the process and not lose your way.

Remember to do things in phases, and you have to get uncomfortable to get results. If you are too comfortable, you won't have a chance to benefit from your crazy faith. Also, take your chances and attend events that will benefit your idea. At these major events, you will meet people that can connect you to your industry. If you are a person who is shy and afraid to talk to people, you have to let that go. When attending a function, walk in the room and own it. Own that person you inspire to be. No one wants to work with someone who is afraid or shy. You have to get to a point where you make yourself so uncomfortable that you will do the very thing you fear. Fear is something you can control. You have to be ten steps ahead of fear every day. Be sure to attend at least two professional development retreats throughout the year. Professional development events will give you the opportunity to find the things you are very good at doing.

Write the name of four to five professional development events that you can attend during the year to enhance your skills. Then, narrow the list down to two that you can attend for the year. Be sure to attend a conference that will challenge you to excel in your industry.

_____

_____

_____

_____

_____

_____

_____

_____

_____

_____

_____

_____

_____

_____

_____

_____

_____

_____

_____

_____

CHAPTER 13
Living Life Abundantly

When you focus on being a blessing, God makes sure that you are always blessed in abundance.

Joel Osteen

Are you truly living an abundant life? When God said He gave you a life to live abundantly, you better believe He did. Some people walk around like they are dead already on this earth. It's as if they are planning a funeral. CONFESSION: That was me for five straight years. Even after my son was born, I didn't have life in me. I was depressed, and my relationship was not making it easier. However, I realized that I had change the way I was thinking if I wanted a better life. I had to shift my mindset to regain ultimate focus on what God wanted from me. Looking for the good in other people has made me realize how much better I can be in life. I learned to level my expectations and treat the good, bad, and ugly the same.

This book is compiled with stories of people that believed in the most unthinkable things, believed in the craziest things, and used crazy faith to trust that everything that they had written down and focused on would come true. The power of putting yourself in a situation to prosper can remove generational curses, poverty, and so much more. God would never give us more than what we can bear.

The best part about believing with crazy faith demonstrates that we understand and believe that all things are possible with God. Your faith can take you from a small space to a mansion. How much are you willing to believe that God will supply all of your needs? As human beings, it's so easy for us to give up. This book was birthed to motivate those that have an idea. It is important to understand that your faith can take you anywhere you want to go. It is how much you are willing to believe that God has the power to make that change for you.

Your commitment is what will allow you to tell your story, and it will help you stand out from the crowd. Furthermore, your commitment to your product and the things you believe in is what allows you to obtain your goals. Commitment will take your faith to another level. Even if you fail a couple of times, your dedication will be your strength.

There are people who like to commit to so many things but nothing that would be beneficial for them. I am God's example of restoration. I remember committing to everything except the things that would allow me to grow. Everyone else had my time except me. Your time is your most valuable asset. What are your goals? Where do you see yourself? How do you plan to get there?

I know you've heard it before, but your attitude will determine your aptitude. If you believe in yourself enough, then you can make improvements in your life. Do not let anyone else determine your worth and your value. Take the first step into a better life by simply believing that great things can happen to you. My mom was the person that I always respected the most. She always dreamed of having a house that she could call hers, and she wanted it to be a place where her children would have a home.

In June 2006, right after I graduated from college, my mom signed on her first house. In the Haitian community, buying a house is a big thing. However, it was the most difficult process that neither of us understood. Nevertheless, she signed on the dotted line and became a first-time home buyer. Let me put it out there that if you never fall, you will never know how to get up. Were there obstacles? Of course. My mom and I didn't even know the difference between property tax and Homestead tax at that time. In fact, we knew nothing about home ownership except that you are supposed to live in the house.

On November 12, 2008, a few weeks before Thanksgiving, an officer came to the door and told me - because my mom wasn't there - that we would have two weeks before we would have to leave the property. I couldn't understand that, because I thought everything was okay. He told me that we had a sale date on the house, and someone else was going to buy the property. I never thought in a million years that my family and I wouldn't have a place to stay. The officer mentioned that our house was foreclosed. I remember that day vividly. I stayed in my car for the rest of the night. I didn't know how to tell my mom that she was losing the piece of the American freedom she had. On top of that, my mom is Haitian, so you have to come with full details before you get dismissed.

After holding on to the papers all night, I said a prayer and asked God not to let this happen to my mother. She'd worked hard to keep her house. Earlier the next day, I showed my mom the papers, and she was devastated. Rule # 1 in a Haitian household: Don't come home with bad news. Don't do it. However, I knew deep down that there was something that could be done.

We reviewed the papers, signed, and mailed them back to the courthouse. Attached to all the documents, I submitted a personal letter to the judge asking him for more time for us to correct whatever was going on with our house. We didn't just sit back and give up.

I started to do research and found out that my mom was being abused by the bank system, so we got an attorney to help my mother. I told myself and my siblings that we would not go out without a fight. It took us almost 2 years to figure things out and to get the judge to overturn the sale date.

You see, my mother worked hard to earn a living. Nothing was given, but much work was required to keep what she worked hard for. June of 2016 marked ten years since my mother stayed in her property. We have a testimony! What if I didn't help my mother? What if we gave up after reviewing the foreclosure notice? Your faith can take you from the streets into a house just like that. I never thought I would have to work so hard to help my mother keep her house. I didn't know anything about the foreclosure process, but I was willing to learn and understand. Crazy faith is about restoring broken homes, broken relationships, messed up marriages, building small businesses, and trusting God with all your heart. God did it!

Challenge yourself today to face fear and look at it dead in the face. You have the power to move, but you choose to settle for mediocrity. We make decisions based on the level of our faith, and for most of us, we are not making the best decisions. When you come across an obstacle, don't think about what you don't have in front of you or how you will obtain the support you need to get there. Through this journey, my mother was able to help other people through the foreclosure process.

I want you to get off your couch or your seat and just do it. Do what you can to change your attitude to get the life you deserve. Most people stay so caught up with where they are they can't see where they are going. Things will get really hard. I know it. This thing we call life is rough, and it will take you six feet under if you are not careful.

If we would have focused on the foreclosure package, we would be sleeping somewhere else right now. Life is about taking chances and daring yourself, even when you can't see the support ahead of you. With faith, you are not supposed to see anything. When you are able to see the things in life, you interfere with your personal development. There will come a time in your life where you will face the most difficult situation. Trust me, the challenges will come. Your comeback power has to be greater than your setbacks. Everything happens for a reason whether you want to believe it or not. Think of some situations in your life that are current setbacks for you. Take some time reflect. Write them down and think of people that can help you with these setbacks. Don't be afraid to ask for help. Now be careful how you ask. Don't sit and complain about your situation. To ask effectively, you have to first be clear about what you want. Remember, to use positive language and speak of future possibility instead.

The major challenges that I am facing are and I plan to overcome them by doing:

_____

_____

_____

_____

_____

_____

_____

_____

_____

_____

_____

_____

_____

_____

*You don't have to master everything,
start where you are today, and do
something.*

Suze Guillaume

CHAPTER 14

The Power of Giving

"The things you do for yourself are gone when you are gone, but the things you do for others remain as your legacy."

Kalu Ndukwe Kalu

If you understand the power of giving, then you will start living an abundant life. Giving isn't something that is forced; it will come naturally. You don't have to give money. You can give your time, you can connect a college student with a mentor, or you can help someone that fell down. You can even pay for someone's gas for their car when you know they don't have it. You can share opportunities on your social media network so that other people can have access to it. Give because that is how your blessings are doubled.

Okay, so people say don't give too much, or you have to make your money for yourself. Yes, that's true. You do need to make sure that you are bringing in income. There has to be a limit to your freebees, but God also says to give. He says to give to the poor, and He will bless us. Give to those in need, and He will bless us. This is where I learned the power of giving.

If we listen closely to the voice inside, we will know exactly what to give and how to give.

There is a lady who worked all her life at a hospital. She loved baking though. She would bake for her church and for community events. Every time she was asked to do something for a community event, she would tell the people to purchase the products and she will bake the items they needed. She never charged the people who were asking for her service. Her love for people and baking is what she was in loved with. People loved her baked goods so much that everyone was contacting her to bake. She created a Facebook page and her fan based grew. Today, this same woman that was working at the hospital is now running a successful baking business online and in Germany. She is now a millionaire teaching other woman in her industry. You got to be bigger than your dreams. This woman was in her late 40's and never thought about the money. This story made me realize the power of giving and the God we serve. I want you to think of two to three organizations or people that you would like to donate to or help. You can include your church. There are so many ways you can give back to your community. You can also give as you grow.

At times, people focus solely on their blessings and don't share with others, the opportunities that God has placed on their hearts. Pay attention closely to how you give and the way you feel when you give. Do you notice a difference when you give more and create opportunities for others to shine? How do you feel when others shine with you? Never think that making it to the top is a solo trip. When God is opening doors for you, He is making room for others to come along. You may not feel that way, but that's how God wants us to feel. Freely give so that blessings can overflow in your life. Make it to the top by helping others.

Think of three or four organizations that you would like to work with to give back, and think about how giving back will benefit what you are doing. Never without understanding why you are giving.

_____

_____

_____

_____

_____

_____

_____

_____

_____

_____

_____

_____

_____

_____

_____

_____

_____

_____

_____

_____

_____

_____

_____

_____

_____

_____

*"As you meet the needs of others, you
will never lack anything."*

Lailah Gifty Akita

CHAPTER 15

The Power of No

How to Reverse Your No into God's Yes!

No! No! No! Everywhere you turn, someone or something is denying you access to greatness. Sadly, you fall for it every time. When someone tells you no, you automatically think that's the end of everything. Instead, you should become immune the word no and let it be your motivation. The power of rejection can change your life and your circumstances. When I am rejected, I begin to push harder than I ever did before. Actually, my son taught me the power of being told no.

I remember when my son was just four years old and he asked me to visit the White House. I can clearly remember telling him that it couldn't happen. I responded this way because I didn't know what it was like to say yes. I was even loud when I told to him that the White House is only for grown-ups. He looked at me with his droopy eyes and said, "Well, you said if I pray, then things will come true." I told him he was right, but the White House would not be possible.

I was really upset at myself after telling him that. How could I, as a parent, teach my son that all things are possible with Christ, but then I turned around and killed his dream? Days went by, and I contacted a close friend to the family and asked if he could help me grant my son's wish. He said my son's dream was farfetched because of the timeframe, but he agreed to give it a shot. My good friend was working on my son's dream. Because of this, my son believed in his heart that he was going to the White House, despite my initial response. He even started to look closer at the map to see where Washington, D.C. was located.

A few days before my son's birthday, I was sitting at my computer at work when I received an email that read: *White House Tour Information Required.* I could barely feel my legs. I opened the email, and it said that EJ was scheduled for a private White House Tour. From there, I knew the power of a NO. Now what would have happened if I had ignored my son? Would I have taught him to say no to everything he desired? I ran throughout my entire workplace because God had answered my son's prayer.

The crazy thing is I always had a passion for writing. After my son's private tour of the White House, I know God gave me like five seats. Yet, a denial is not always a bad thing. Allow yourself to accept denials. Now, let me explain that before my son got approved to visit the White House, he got denied. They gave us some random excuse about the White House not having anymore more tickets. Well, they must have been out of their minds to tell me no.

I started to call everyone I could think of to get my son's wish granted. You see, denial doesn't really mean no. Some people just deny because they can. God says to speak Him and He will give you the answers. Lord knows I never fasted so hard in my life. God answered our prayers. If you think for one second you serve a little God, then go ahead and dream as far as your eyes can see clearly.

Write out those things or situations that you must learn to say no to, and the reasons why you must.

_____

_____

_____

_____

_____

_____

_____

_____

_____

_____

_____

_____

CHAPTER 16

Get to Work!

If You Are on an Assignment to Do Something,

Doing big things doesn't mean that you have to start your vision by borrowing thousands of dollars to move your ideas. You can start small, but you have to have big dreams and big ideas. Yes, your dreams have to be bigger than you. You have to believe in yourself to make that big idea happen. Doing it big does require you to put it in work. There is no idea that will move on its own. Your ideas are worth an action plan that you will work for. There was a young man that had a vision at the age of nineteen, but he had no guidance. His vision was valid, but he had no money to support his project. So he started to save the money that he would get from the financial aid office and from scholarships.

He realized if he would start saving, he could really start working on his dream. He didn't even wait until he had a large amount of money saved before he got started. He had a vision to start a business, he believed in his product, and he knew that it would work. Therefore, he started right where he knew he could with his friends and at his college campus.

He started to use the resources he had by connecting with mentors and leaders that would come on campus to speak. He had a passion for design and construction. He connected with a gentleman that had an architecture firm and started to volunteer at the firm. On the side, he started a business where people could call his firm to find the best architects and construction companies to build and fix homes. He didn't need a license for that, but he needed his faith. In his business, he would contract the best firms, and he used his company to help construction businesses get contracts in his state. He graduated from college years later. Now, he has a growing firm, and he has worked alongside the greatest in the business.

What does it take for you to believe in yourself? How much of us walk around knowing our purpose and worth? I want to tell you that you are worth it. Regardless of the obstacles and circumstances, your gifts and abilities are worth giving a try. If he never tried, he would have never known his worth on this earth. You have to get to work, even if you can't see how you are going to accomplish your goals. Faith is not something that you can physically see. Moreover, crazy faith is definitely something you can't see - not even when you create a plan knowing where you are going. You have enough power in you to change your circumstances. Are you willing to put in the work?

I want you to write down three business ideas that you have in mind. Yes, write it down. Get in the habit of writing down your ideas. Stop allowing your visions and abilities to go to waste. Most of us sit at our 9-5 jobs praying for change to happen. Start using what you have to make the best out of your situation. Don't rely on your boss to help you make that move. Don't rely on your friends to help you make that move. In fact, reevaluate the people you have on your team. The friends you have in your circle can help you move to the next level. Do what you have to do to get the work done. What will be your next move? I dare you to dream bigger than yesterday. The time that you dedicated to your day job should be the same time you dedicate to your passion and your vision.

I have heard it all before. Stop comparing yourself to people that have nothing to do with you. God made you just how He wanted to make you. There is nothing to worry about. Start thinking of your next move, and start making plans to change your circumstances. If you don't do what is right for you, no one else will do it for you. On earth, we all have a purpose and an assignment to complete. There is someone waiting on you to complete the task.

Deep down, you know what needs to be done, put that into writing and act!

_____

_____

_____

_____

_____

_____

_____

_____

_____

_____

_____

_____

_____

_____

_____

_____

*Take action. It's the only thing
separating you from your dreams.*

Lisa Nichols

CHAPTER 17

Capitalizing on Opportunity

A pessimist sees the difficulty in every opportunity; an optimist sees the opportunity in every difficulty.

Winston Churchill

As a little girl, I learned how to **capitalize on opportunity**. Have you ever been asked to participate in an event and not get paid? (I have both hands up.) Now, I don't sit around saying yes to every invitation, but I find the opportunities that fit what I am doing, and I capitalize on it. I know sometimes it is easy to say decline a gig or an opportunity where you are not getting paid or benefiting, but try to come up with a success plan to reap the benefits of the opportunity.

If it is a speaking engagement, see if you can sell your products and waive the speaking fee to help nonprofit organizations. Your goal is to build your network and the people you come across. I know we all want to make money for our services, but sometimes you can leverage that chance and make it bigger than you ever dreamed. See, God has placed most of the blessings right in front of us, and we can't see them because we are looking for the wrong things.

When looking at opportunities, figure out who the audience will be, the amount of people attending, the representation of the organization, and how you can align yourself or your product with what you are doing. Don't be afraid to take chances. Be confident with the decisions that you make. There are times when you will have to turn things down. Still, for the most part, understand how you can capitalize on opportunities.

The best way is to do the research and find out the events that are taking place in your community and how you can participate. At many events, remember that you are there to network and connect with people. It also helps to build a relationship with the people you meet so that you can identify their role in their perspective industry. Also, be sure to connect with people after each event. I would send an email that said it was nice to meet them, and I would love to stay connected. When sending emails to someone you met at a special event, keep your email short and sweet. I have gotten so many quick responses.

This is called capitalizing on opportunities. Most of these people are connected with someone in a particular industry that interests you. Every time you are at networking event, maximize the time you're spending at the event. Furthermore, be sure to set a goal of how many people you would like to meet. The same thing goes for a student in college. You want to connect people with the industry. Also, remember to never stop coming up with new content, new ideas, and new products. We all are creative in some way or another. When you have one thing going, you want to keep the momentum by producing more content.

Always remember that partnerships also can benefit you when you are capitalizing on opportunity. Partnering with organizations helps you put two minds or perspectives together. Your goal is to always grow and not stop at one venture. Continue to develop new ideas and master them. As you become strong at one, start developing the next. I don't think God put us on this earth to live ordinary lives. We have enough power to ignite our own opportunity.

I would never be where I am today if I didn't capitalize on opportunities. You have to know a good thing when you see it. You have to be able to analyze and see something amazing. When people would ask me to do a workshop or to speak on a panel, I would say to myself that I have never done that before. Yet, I still seized the opportunity.

Don't worry about how you are going to reach your goal. That should be the last thing on your mind. Some people say you need to create a business plan and have some blueprint as to where you are going. Not really… In fact, some people spend so much time trying to figure out the business plan that they never get started on the idea. Stop trying to figure things out, and just do it. Social media has allowed so many people to build their platform. Place your idea a page, and start connecting with your target audience. Your contributions matter more than anything. Everything you will do for others you will leave behind with your legacy. Find out what you are passionate about, and get to work. You can't be comfortable where you are.

Brace yourself for a new chapter of your life, continue to conquer your fears, and make things happen. I didn't know I was going to release a book this year. I knew I wanted to write something to get people off their bottoms and to stop complaining. Nothing comes to people who sit and wait for something to happen for them. After becoming ill, I could have gone into a pity party feeling bad for myself. Instead, I started to get involve with causes that interested me. I am sharing what I know to inspire people to move past their fears.

As you start to grow, you will realize that other people are growing around you. You need to decide today if you are ready and willing to make the next move. I would like for you to take a break and reflect on the next couple of months. Do you plan to attend some upcoming functions? Think of four to five networking events you can attend or create within the next five months. It can be a social gathering for professional working millennial, and so much more.

Describe the five events below. Then, connect with the event coordinators to see if there are any partnership opportunities. Also, write down what you plan on getting out of the networking events. There should always be a goal on how you can share your product. Always be prepared for an opportunity.

Think of three networking events you can attend that will benefit your ideas. Think of people you can connect with that will help you get there and make it happen.

_____

_____

_____

_____

_____

_____

_____

_____

_____

_____

_____

_____

_____

_____

_____

_____

_____

_____

_____

_____

_____

_____

_____

_____

_____

_____

_____

"Lack of direction, not lack of time, is the problem. We all have twenty-four hour days."

Zig Ziglar

CHAPTER 18
Keep on Knocking

"Persist and persevere, and you will find most things that are attainable, possible."

Philip Stanhope

Your goal is to keep on knocking. Yes, keep on knocking until that door opens. Knock until your hands fall off. If you want something, you have to put in work. Oh, and you can't just accept anything. Be persistent and consistent with your mission. We give up too easily. Some of us get so discouraged when someone slams the door in our face. It's okay if that happens. A rejection is just getting your closer to the time of acceptance. Keep knocking on doors that are closed. The people behind the closed doors will not be there forever. The road ahead is tough, but you have to be able to handle the tough times. There will be times you will look in the mirror and realized that you have no resources or support. However, you must keep going. You have to look past the obstacles.

A young mother that I met a couple of years back was twenty-seven years old in college with a reading level of a second grader. She was going to college, and she was clueless. The reason why she decided to go to college was because her husband said he would support her. She was scared for her life to go back to school. She couldn't read anything, and everything seemed blurred to her.

Even though she was diagnosed with a disability, she still pushed herself to go to college. When she would do her homework, she would ask her kids who were in elementary school to help her. She created her own dictionary with her own words, because she couldn't seem to understand the Webster dictionary. I know this is different and strange, but she did what worked for her. I can only imagine what she went through trying to understand the lessons in her classes. Still, she didn't give up.

She took advantage of tutoring on her college campus and studied an extra three hours a day, because she knew that the average student studied maybe five hours a week. Toward the end of her program, she went to her counselor and wanted to make sure she would meet the requirements for graduation. Although, she knew that it would be challenging, she did it. It took her almost three and a half years to finish her degree.

To make the process easier, she used every resource on campus to help her pass her classes. She even found organizations on campus that help students with math anxiety. Her dream is to become a nurse, and she is now one step closer to achieving her dream. She continued to knock on every door until someone would help and not judge her reading level. She accomplished what most people say they can't do, and what some people think is almost impossible to complete. I was so proud of her. She even got accepted into nursing school!

Sometimes we allow our limits to cause us to be so still that we do not achieve our goals. What do you think forced her to act? Sometimes life will force you to act even when you don't want to move. Our greatest gift is our faith. It's the one thing we can control. If you allow yourself to believe that something is possible, then you can control that. God has given you that power over your life to make things happen for yourself.

I want you to start thinking of a dream or an idea that you placed on hold because you think it's impossible. Is it the idea of going to law school? Is it the idea to write a book? Is it the will to speak at a conference? Your dreams are necessary. Sometimes we get so caught up living in other people's dreams that our own dreams are needed to empower other people. I challenge you to repeat the affirmations below daily:

- ♥ My dreams are necessary.

- ♥ My success benefits all those around me.

- ♥ My faith will guide my thoughts.

- ♥ I can turn my weaknesses into my strength.

- ♥ If I push myself, I can make it happen.

- ♥ My assignment has a purpose.

- ♥ I will, I can, I must.

- ♥ No one can determine my value.

- ♥ With God, all things are possible.

- ♥ Challenges will make me stronger.

CHAPTER 19

Instrument of Change

*If you don't like something, change it.
If you can't change it, change your
attitude.*

Maya Angelou

What does it take to be an instrument of change? It takes you stepping out on faith and believing that your vision and your mission are not about you. It's about that little girl who never had that one person to read a book with her. It's about that little boy who wants to be the President of the United States when he grows up. You are one step closer to making a difference in someone's life. You are an instrument of change. You are who God created to make a difference in the world.

Social media allows us to connect with people that we would probably never see a day in our lives. However, you have the power to influence so many people every day of your life – even without social media. What you choose to do with your time is essential to how you can change the world. People around you may not understand how they can influence those around them, because they are concerned with what they don't have. You have all that you need through your voice to be the change of the world. You can influence young people around you. You can host events at your local library or community center. You can start your organization to benefit the children or elders in your community.

About two years ago, I met a young girl online who created a group on social media to connect women who were brand new entrepreneurs that need more resources to build their businesses. At one point the members of the group were traveling together and networking outside of social media. They even started a monthly empowerment call to encourage each other to stay on track. How do you think this one person was able to influence so many people? Now she is running a million-dollar business. In addition, the women in her group started to grow as well. Can you be an instrument of change? You don't need anyone's validation to determine the worth of your vision. You don't need validation from your family or social media likes and shares. If it's God's purpose and will for you, then everything will happen naturally.

Take the time to think of ways that you can make a difference in your community. You can start anywhere. Find the organizations that inspire you and find people who will inspire you. Remember, don't be afraid to ask. Write the names of the organizations and search for contacts. Be sure to follow up with your connections.

_____

_____

_____

_____

_____

_____

_____

_____

_____

_____

_____

_____

"Whatever the mind can conceive and believe, it can achieve."

Napoleon Hill*, Think and Grow Rich*

CHAPTER 20

Releasing Your Emergency Brake

*Success is not final, failure is not fatal: it
is the courage to continue that counts.*

Winston Churchill

Before you continue reading, please take your foot off
the emergency brake. We often keep a sob story in
the bag in case of an emergency. Then, we pull the
emergency brake when we need someone to feel sorry for us.
Stop playing the victim in everything you do. You have to
try some things and fail some times. Believe it or not, failure
is not a bad thing. It doesn't even mean that you will not
make it nor does it mean that you have damaged your entire
life. Don't let it stop you from taking chances and making
sacrifices. Moreover, don't let failure force you to coast
through life with your foot prepared to make an emergency
stop. When you have your foot on the emergency brakes,
you begin to question everything, and God doesn't like that.

Some of us miss out on opportunities because our faith is so weak.

I had my foot on the emergency brake for a long time because I couldn't trust people around me. It was rare to find someone who would push me go harder. I felt like every man was for himself. Therefore, I no longer sought the approval or support of others. I started to trust my own decisions, and I was taking more risks - even if I knew the plan didn't make sense. I worried less about the problem and focused more on solution. I never worried how I was going to start a publishing company or who was going to direct my path. Releasing my emergency brakes allowed me to see a new me. It also allowed me to see the power God gave me to live with crazy faith. When I started the publishing company I only had $30 to start. Did I doubt the idea, of course I did; however, I kept pushing.

Press through the rejections and the negative people that try to bring you down. The power of reading and writing has taken my son to so many places that he only imagined. Do you know the plan God has for you? Do you trust that God will lead you in the right direction? Emergency brakes are clearly just another road block you to stop WHAT YOU ARE DOING. There are times when we need emergency brakes. On the other hand, sometimes we have it locked down to the point that we forget that we can move by releasing our fears.

Take a break and review any major setback in your life or anything you are afraid of doing. After that, write down five things that can help you overcome that fear. Repeat it every day. You have to adapt better to change and support each other. If I can do it, so can you. I'm God's vessel being used to move you from *I wish* to *I'm doing it.*

_____

_____

_____

_____

_____

_____

_____

_____

_____

_____

_____

_____

_____

_____

_____

_____

_____

_____

_____

_____

CHAPTER 21
Trust the Process

*If you can't describe what you are doing
as a process, you don't know what you're
doing.*

W. Edwards Deming

Sitting in a dark four-wall room at the age of twenty-seven was nerve-wracking. I thought my entire life is over. The room felt to be about eighty something degrees or maybe I was going through some kind of menopause. Moments later, I had to endure a major pain. I had one hand holding on to a Kit-Kat bar, and the other hand holding on to the most uncomfortable bed. Suddenly, I went from a dark room to a room filled with high beam lights as if the sun was shining on me. After the most uncomfortable push, I heard a voice crying extremely loud.

It was the voice of my little man. We both looked at each other and cried to the point where the doctor started crying.

I thought to myself, *"What I am going to do with a baby. I have no money, and this wasn't planned."* However, I had given birth to an angel. It was the most difficult process, but my son became the healing that I needed in my life. I know he was probably thinking, *"What am I doing in this place with this woman?"* Don't worry we both feel the same son. Meanwhile, I was thinking to myself that there had to be more to life.

I didn't want my son growing up living in fear. I want more for him. I told God that no matter what happens, I want to place my son in His hands. That would keep me from being afraid of where I was going. After that, I started to analyze my surroundings, and I got rid of things that were holding me back. I needed to do more. I thought going back to college would have solved that problem, but I opted against that idea after the birth of my child.

I saved the money that I got from my income tax refund to purchase a professional camera. Then, I started taking pictures. I used YouTube to learn the fundamentals of photography. I practiced every day with my family and anything that had legs. Then, my friends and family started to ask me to take pictures for them. They would ask me how much were my packages, and I had to research to understand what they meant. I would ask them to give me what I deserve, and then I realize that was not working out.

Therefore, I created small packages to offer photography services to family and friends.

I will never forget the day I got paid almost $2,500 to do photography for a big wedding. I had to tell God that I don't think I deserved that much money. I didn't even think people would believe that I could actually get the work done. Nevertheless, after that big wedding, I began to trust the process. I started to trust the journey that I was on in life. I started to pay attention to details in my life, and I started to remove negative things.

I was going somewhere with photography. It was taking me somewhere that I had never been. I stopped listening to my critics, and I began to open up my secret box that held my crazy faith. I started believing that all things were possible because God said that I am worth it. I started to become more serious about photography, and I focused on learning the process. I developed so many skills while learning, and I loved it.

Are you sitting around not knowing what your talents are? Is there something that you are good at that you can turn from a hobby to an official business? What gift and talents are you running from each day? The moment I discovered my talents, I told God that I had to trust Him. Begin to move without questioning your faith. Find out the things that you are good at and make moves. We question our abilities so much that we lose out on opportunities. Start thinking of things that you never thought you could do, and think about the things that will motivate you to focus on that hidden talent. After focusing on that talent, continue to master it. Get better by practicing every day, and by trusting the process.

I had to trust that I would birth a healthy baby boy, and I had to trust that my gifts would save my life. Before my son, I never thought that anything was possible for me. Consequently, I was quitting everything. I would start something and never finish it. I'm not here to bore you about my life, but I want you to find greatness in yourself. You've got it. Below, I want you to write five things you could be good at doing. It could be anything. As an alternative, you can write something down that you always dreamed about doing. I believe in the power of words and writing down my ideas. It has changed my life and my thought process. I know that when you write your ideas down, it will help you identify the things that you can master.

You don't have to share your thoughts with anyone. After you have written them down, I want you to circle one thing that you can focus on today. Don't move on to the next page without working on this assignment. So many people want to get ahead in life, but they don't want to do the work. Stop whatever you are doing, and focus on you right now. That one item that you will circle may be that one thing that will change your life for the next ten years. I DARE YOU TO WORK FOR SUCCESS. You GOT THIS! Stop dreaming. Your time is now!

I am good at doing the following:

_____

_____

_____

_____

_____

_____

_____

_____

_____

_____

_____

_____

_____

_____

_____

_____

_____

_____

_____

CHAPTER 22

Stay on Course

*People with goals succeed because they
know where they're going.*

Earl Nightingale

So many people want to skip the experience so they
can get straight to the blessings. However, it's
necessary to go through the experience to build your
strength. The title of the book is *Do It Big*. What it really
means is to do something, anything to the fullest. Don't wait
on life to do it for you. The experience is the best part of life.
When I started working for MTV, I didn't know that the
opportunity would prepare me for my future. It was a great
experience. In fact, I almost turned down the opportunity
because I didn't really know if it was something that I could
do.

After that, I began saying yes to every opportunity that
would help me get closer to the career that I was interested

in starting. My experiences were necessary to make me a winner. Winners will get up and win every day and forget about doubting their journey. I remember the day that I was about to give up, and I will never forget it. It happened to be the darkest moment in my life. I went to visit my dentist because I was feeling this major pain in my gums. I thought I was losing all my teeth.

The doctor told me that there was a tumor underneath my nose. In my mind, I could only think of three words… MY HAITIAN PARENTS. See, I told them something was wrong with me when I was young. I had a tumor that was stopping my teeth from growing in at all. From the time I was in the third grade, I never had my two front teeth. I went to middle school, high school, and college with no front teeth. You know what that means, no smiling for any graduation pictures.

The dentist told me that I had a tumor the entire time. I was depressed. Then, he said I needed a major surgery done as soon as possible. It was the worse time of my life. After my major surgery, I was home for almost three months recovering and sipping from cups. I had a great deal of soup, too. However, I realized how important it was to stay on course even through the pain. Stay on course simply means to pursue your goals, regardless of the obstacles.

After recovery, my orthodontists used a chain they called an anchor to help bring down my teeth that were hidden underneath my nose for all those years. When my teeth finally came in, I was smiling everywhere. I had a smile again. The last time I smiled like that was when I was only seven years old.

During my recovery process, I never gave up. I started to do work in my community to empower young people to embrace who they are. Always remember that even in your darkest moments, you have to stay focused. If I focused more on the tumor, I wouldn't have made it out of that hard time in my life. I share this story to tell you that no matter what you are going through, there is a light at the end of the tunnel. Have you ever been in a difficult situation that caused you to lose your faith? If you're in a season of giving up, lean in. Trust the loving hands of God to bring you back to your place of peace.

Someone out there needs your gift. Keep pushing through difficult times. Don't delay. Stay on course. Set Goals. You have greatness within you.

Think of a time when you just wanted to give up. It's important to remember those moments. Write down the things that helped you get out of your situation.

_____

_____

_____

CHAPTER 23

Using Your Resources

When you believe in your dream and your vision, then it begins to attract its own resources. No one was born to be a failure.

Myles Munroe

I've learned a very important lesson from my mentors, and that is to use every resource possible especially those that you can access. You can continue to use your resources and build meaningful relationships. There are many times when we don't pay attention to details because we're focused on trying to make money. However, you don't have to be rich to see an opportunity before you. In truth, you don't need all the money in the world. Still, some of us over think things too much, and we try to analyze every obstacle that we face. You just need to apply the resources that you have to what you are doing. It's that simple. There are so many people that I can connect with to help me get to where I need to go. I am grateful because I have been able to connect with so many people.

While you are using your resources it's also best to build long-lasting relationships. Don't just use people to get to where you want to go. Interact and get to know them. Support their event and engage in dialogue. Using your resources means connecting with the people in your network that will support your ideas. It doesn't always mean that you have to spend loads of money. Though, you do want to invest in your professional development. I found out which people I knew who had written a book, and I connected with them. I did research, extended greetings, and welcomed to editors to help me with the process. I never questioned if they would ignore me, because all that matters is that I reached out to them.

CHAPTER 24

Invest in Yourself

"Your mind is your greatest asset, enrich it."

O. E Moshe

Many times when you are planning a special event, you may request sponsors and ask people to donate. However, it is important for you to fund your own project. You have to believe in your project first. Most people want big companies to sponsor them right away, but that company has no way to trust that your vision is worth their donation. You have to the value your work before someone else can see it for you. How much do you think your idea is worth? The smartest thing to do is to invest in your own project, but call in help if and only when necessary, without relinquishing control. That is the power of crazy faith. If someone would show you what crazy faith looks like, you would ever think small again. I'm not saying to go and run and get a $10,000 loan to fund your idea, but you have to know the worth of your project. You know what it will take to move on your idea.

I started my son's book project with $30. I told myself that my son had a vision, and I had to support him. I invested in his idea because I knew it would be worth it in the end. His dream was necessary, and it was something that I knew would change his way of thinking. When you allow God to take the lead, you will see that your vision and ideas were not even meant for you. I knew firsthand that I had God's permission to be great when I started believing that all things were possible. The God we serve is real. I promise He won't let you down. You are worth the investment. You don't have to run around chasing people to fund your dreams. You got this. Look where I am at with a $30 investment. I even have a confident child, too. What a difference your faith can make in your life!

CHAPTER 25
Don't take it Personally

On your journey to success, don't put all of your trust in people and don't take things personally. People that you interact with are human beings, and they are not mind readers. There will be some people that want to help you and others who won't. It's not because they don't want to help. It's that most people wait to see the end result of your success. Once they see everything working out for you, they will try to jump on the bandwagon and say they were there or ask how they can support. You have to motivate yourself every day, and you can't expect people to believe in your dream more than you. You have to make your dreams work.

I learned that there are three groups of people when you are working on your visions. The first group will support you from far away. They may like a few things on your social media pages, but that's all you will get. Now, they are not bad people, but that is how they support. They will cheer you on, but they won't invest in your idea. The second group will like everything you do and share your idea. This second group may take a little longer to support your idea with money. The third group is the group that will share, connect you with people that will help you, and they will invest in your idea and/or purchase your product. The third group is a limited group, but this is the group of people that you want to invest in you. Keep the names of those people close and don't let them go. You will be surprised at the outpour of support that you will receive from them.

In essence, don't take things personally when people don't give you a 100% support. Your goal is to make sure you are reaching the people that need to hear your story or have access to your product. Share your story until you have reached the people you intended to reach. If someone doesn't purchase your product, don't focus on that. You have enough great things going for you than for you to waste time to worry about what other people are not doing. You can only control what you do. You owe it to yourself to be great. I believe in you. I know God put us on this earth to live an abundant life, and I trust that your success will touch the lives of many.

In addition, your faith will allow you to see things that you never thought you would see. Don't sweat the small stuff, because that's all they are - small things that you can't control. Some people may be fighting a battle that you don't even know about. Determine your worth now, and give God the glory for opening your eyes to a new life that you and your family deserve.

CHAPTER 26

Embrace Your Fears and Act on Faith

When you embrace your fears, you will begin to accept your journey. Fears can stall your blessings and your assignments. We all have an assignment that God want us to complete. I know you are probably wondering what your assignment is; just ask God and He will reveal it to you. Don't rush him. Some people don't even know they have an assignment to complete in life. If you know your fears, you can learn to act on faith. My biggest fear was speaking to people. I used to attend event and I would sit in a dark corner until it was time for me to go. What was my purpose for being there in the first place? I didn't even realize that I wasted precious time at the event.

Someone out there that needed to hear about what I was doing didn't even get a chance to hear me because of my fear. This changed after I left high profile event with so many key people. When I got home, I sat down in my room and made a list of fears that I had. I mean I wrote down everything I could think of that I was afraid of doing. After writing the list of things, I made a separate list of things that could help me overcome those fears. After reviewing my list, I realized that my faith had more power. I decided that I was not going to give my fears any power. Likewise, I started to put more emphasis on my best attributes. I love meeting new people and that definitely helped me open up to people more.

Realize that every connection and interaction with a person can bring you closer to your blessings. Now it's your turn to write down your fears. This is your book, and you have a journal in it. So you can write down anything. Jot down at least five fears. Then, write down ten things that will help you overcome each fear. After writing these items, I want you to review them and read the affirmations after your list. Repeat to yourself again. As a result of this exercise, you are going to bury your fears and live the life you deserve. Read more books that can empower you. Listen to motivational videos that can empower you. You have to get up, move on your dreams, and work for success. When you see your list of fears again, you will bury them with your mind and never give them the opportunity to live again.

CHAPTER 27

Know Your Why

"Some men have thousands of reasons why they cannot do what they want to, when all they need is one reason why they can."

Martha Graham

Why do you want to do big things and be successful? The part where people fail the most is the fact that their *why* is not greater. I told God that when He takes me, I want to leave the world empty. I want to give people the same opportunity I had to grow. Maybe that is why I'm so passionate about what I do. My *why* is very simple and straight to the point. I want my son to look at his life and say that his mom taught him how to work for success.

Being a single mom has been the most challenging experience for me. It also gave me my strength and taught me exactly what my mom was going through with me. It has also been the best experience, I learned exactly what God wanted me to learn through it. I learned to trust God more than ever before. In essence, my *why* has been to give my son a better life than I had and to please my father in Heaven. That's it.

It was one random night when I realized that God wanted me to live for Him. I also realized where my crazy ideas are coming from all this time. As I got closer to Him, my faith became stronger. I didn't have to look to anyone for peace, because I found it.

Your *why* will push you when you get knocked down. Your *why* will wipe your tears away and give you hope again. It's okay to fall, but your *why* will make your comeback stronger. Never drop your head when you come to a lost. Even when things are not going well for you, make someone else smile. Make someone else know that there is hope for them. Your *why* will get you where you need to go, and it will feed your appetite for success. Your effort will allow you to develop a strong backbone that will shape you when you have no push left in you. I've been there before, and I don't plan on going back.

A few years back, I met a man from my dad's church that owned an ice cream truck. I mean he was running a successful ice cream truck business in Miami for over 20 years. He would literally drive this truck 6 days out of the week to sell the best ice cream and fried chicken. He was an older man. His wife would prepare the fried chicken on the truck while he would drive and play the famous ice cream truck music to let people know he was on his way. One day I had the courage to ask him why. Why did he consider this to be a business? He said to me that he always envisioned giving his children the opportunities he didn't have as a child. He said this successful business allowed him to put not one but 3 of kids through college. At that point, I knew that his *Why* was bigger than the ice cream truck.

In a few years, I plan on opening up this book again to review my notes and all of the information I shared with you that changed my life. If I can go back and revisit my graduation day from high school, I would revisit the goals that I had at that time. They were different then, but God's timing is perfect. This book release and the fact that you are reading it have happened in perfect timing. We serve an awesome God, and even if you are not a religious person, you can still trust God.

Allow your comeback to be stronger than your fall. I would be lying if I said that I have a perfect life, because I don't. I only made a commitment to myself to never go back to my past and to focus primarily on my *why* and my future. You have to do the same. Pain is temporary. Everything that came to harm you is temporary. That same pain is going to take you to the next level. On the other side of your life, there is a reward waiting for you. Therefore, let your *why* get you to that reward. Go and prove your enemies wrong by working for success. Remember that everyone will be tested. How strong are you? How strong is that *why*? Below, I want you to write down five *whys* that will help you during your hard times. They will also help you to your road for success.

It doesn't matter what they are, just write them down. Be sure to save this book so that you can look back and examine your progress later. Your dreams have to be bigger than your reality. Don't stop breathing. Don't give up. Also, keep in mind that God is not going to just drop your blessings on your lap. Believe in yourself and work for what you want.

What are your *whys*?

_____

_____

_____

_____

_____

_____

_____

_____

_____

_____

_____

_____

_____

_____

_____

_____

*"The man who moves a mountain begins
by carrying away small stones."*

Confucius: *The Analects*

CHAPTER 28

Turning Your Struggles into Strengths

*Only in art will the lion lie down with
the lamb, and the rose grow without the
thorn.*

Martin Amis

Despite the struggles in your life, your struggles and challenges are necessary. Take advantage of each struggle and turn them into positive affirmations. Remember, you are not your struggles, and you have the power to shape your future through your struggles.

On June 17, 2016, I was on my way to the United State of Women Summit in Washington, DC. It was the first summit ever hosted by President Barack Obama and First Lady Michelle Obama. When I received the email that I was nominated to attend, I realize that it must be an opportunity that I couldn't turn down. I told my family the good news, and they were excited for me. I got on my flight, and off I was to the trip that I would never forget. This was not my first time going to Washington, D.C., but for some reason, it was difficult finding a hotel. I got to the airport around 11:00 p.m. and searching for a hotel was becoming a burden. By 3:00 a.m., I still had no hotel. That's when it finally dawned on me that I didn't have anywhere to go, nor did I have anyone to call at that hour.

During that time at the airport, I met a driver for the airport. He said that he'd lived in D.C. for twenty years. He said there was one hotel that he knew might have a room. We drove to the hotel, but it was booked when we got there. I gave up and told the driver to take me back to the airport. I would rest there for an hour, and then I'd wake up and prepare for the big event. I had to think to myself through that lonely building. I wondered how people who are helpless do it. How do people that are homeless deal with their situation? I was too tired to come up with answers, but I realized that God wanted me to go through this situation. I accepted whatever it was, and an hour later, I was getting dressed in a public bathroom with no shower to attend the biggest event of my life.

When I arrived, there were over five thousand women in the line. All I could think of was the wrinkle dress that I was wearing and that I survived the morning. I had to get over my obstacles really quickly because I was about to meet some pretty cool people. As I entered the Walter E. William Convention Center, I could only think of how blessed I was. So many women from all over the world were coming together for one cause, and that was the #StateofWomen hosted by the White House.

I was a nominated change-maker, and I was taking every second in as if it was my last visit to D.C. Women were everywhere, and the speakers were lined up. The song that played over and over again was *Who Run the World* by Beyonce. My dreams and what I wanted to gain from the summit played in my mind continually. My goal was to meet and connect with five people and to take notes while listening to the speakers.

I got the opportunity to hear President Barack Obama, First Lady Michelle Obama, Vice President Joe Biden, and Oprah Winfrey all speak. I never felt so full in my life! It was a blessing to attend such an amazing summit. The sound of women cheering loudly filled the room. During the event, I ended up with media, and by the end, of the event I made it back stage. I must say that the best food was back stage with Mr. President himself. I started to share my story with the organizers of the event, and I realized that my struggle getting to D.C. was my story that was making me stronger.

This event made me realize that God will make room for his children. He is making room for you now. You know that job that you've been dreaming about, yes, that one, God is making room for you. You know that house you've been dreaming about for years, yes, that one, God is making room for you. However, the most important part of your journey is your faith. Yes, your crazy faith! God want you to trust him. Your relationship with him will be the reason things start to fall in place.

This trip was a huge lesson for me, because I really wanted to grab my bags and leave D.C., but I made the best of it. I ended up speaking to Shonda Rhimes, and I didn't even know it was her (because I don't watch much television). Nevertheless, I will never forget The State of Women Summit. It reminded me that our work is not done, and we are just getting started. Michelle Obama said it best she said to value what you do and do it well. Whatever it takes for you to love what you do, do it. This is how I was able to turn my struggle into my story and my story into my strength.

*"Without ambition one starts nothing.
Without work one finishes nothing. The
prize will not be sent to you. You have to
win it."*

Ralph Waldo Emerson

Excuse me while I praise God on this entire page!

He did it!

Now it is time for you to live out loud. Are you ready? If you are not ready, you need to pass the torch to someone else. I need people who are willing to move despite setbacks and roadblocks. I need people who dare to be different and challenge every obstacle they will face. *Do it Big* is not just a statement, it is who we need to become. Our ideas need to be big, our CRAZY FAITH needs to be big, and OUR work for success needs to be on another level.

Start living out loud and trust that God will open doors. This book is dedicated to my sisters who've been living in fear for so long. I told you that God had a special gift for you. I'm so glad that I had the opportunity to share *DO IT BIG* with you. This is the birth of my second baby. It's the gift that God told me was not mine. It is for someone out there who needs to hear the story. I pray that this book will motivate you to live past your fears.

#DOITBIG

"There is no greater gift you can give or receive then to honor your calling. It's why you were born. And how you become most truly alive."

Oprah Winfrey

Made in the USA
Middletown, DE
17 October 2016